Art's Alive!

What is a Sculpture?

Anne Civardi

SEA-TO-SEA
Mankato Collingwood London

This edition first published in 2006 by
Sea-to-Sea Publications
1980 Lookout Drive
North Mankato
Minnesota 56003

Copyright © Sea-to-Sea Publications 2006

Printed in China

Library of Congress Cataloging-in-Publication Data:

Civardi, Anne
    What is sculpture? / by Anne Civardi
        p. cm. — (Art's alive!)
    Includes index.
    ISBN 1-932889-87-6
    1. Sculpture—Juvenile literature. I. Title. II. Art's alive! (North Mankato, Minn.)
    NB1143.C585 2005
    730—dc22

                                                                2004062513

9 8 7 6 5 4 3 2

Published by arrangement with the Watts Publishing Group Ltd, London

Editor: Caryn Jenner
Design: Sphere Design
Art director: Jonathan Hair
Picture research: Diana Morris

The publisher wishes to thank Fiona Cole for her assistance in making this book.

Acknowledgments:
Arte & Immagini Srl/Corbis: 10. Peter Beck/Corbis: 18. Trustees of the British Museum: 8cr.
© Barry Flanagan, courtesy Waddington Galleries. Exhibited at the New Centre Sculpture Park & Gallery,
Roche Park: 8cl. Kevin Fleming/Corbis: front cover cl, 19r. UKGovernment Art Collection © Andy
Goldsworthy: 23 Ice Star (Scaur Water, Penpont, Dumfriesshire). Robert Harding Picture Library © the artist:
27. Jan Isachen/Images de France/Alamy. © ADAGP, Paris & DACS, London 2004: 15. Gail
Mooney/Corbis: 9. The work illustrated on the front cover, p 17 and p 28 has been reproduced by permission
of the Henry Moore Foundation. © Henry Moore Foundation. Museum Ludwig, Cologne. © ADAGP, Paris
& DACS, London 2004: front cover r: 21. Private Collection. © ARS, New York & DACS, London 2004: 25.
Private Collection/Bridgeman Art Library: 7. Josph Sohm/Corbis: 26. Wakefield Museums & Galleries, West
Yorkshire/Bridgeman Art Library. © Bowness, Hepworth Estate: 11.

Additional photographs taken by Ray Moller.

Every attempt has been made to clear copyright. Should there be any inadvertent omission please apply to
the publisher for rectification.

Contents

What is a sculpture?

A sculpture is a work of art that you can see all the way around. A person who makes a sculpture is called a sculptor.

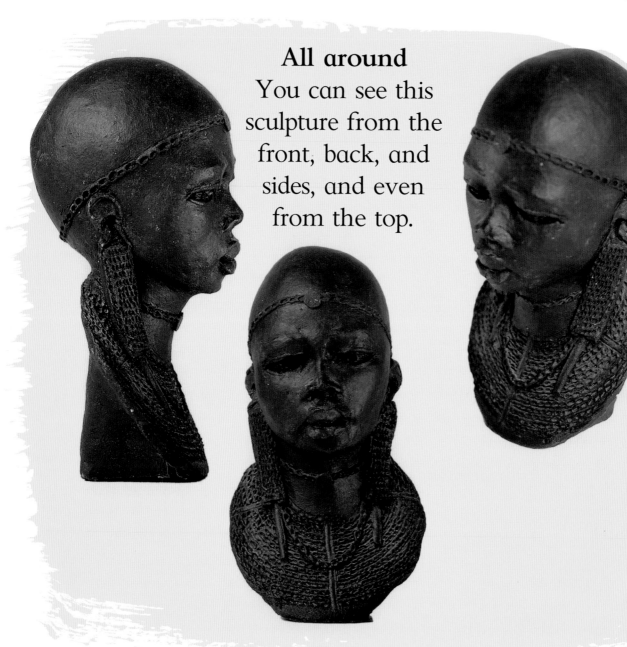

All around
You can see this sculpture from the front, back, and sides, and even from the top.

Degas wanted his sculpture to look like a real ballerina. She is even wearing real clothes!

The Little Dancer Aged Fourteen, **Edgar Degas, 1879-81**
Sculptors use all sorts of materials, such as **clay**, stone, or wood, to make their sculptures. This sculpture is made from a metal called **bronze**.

Where to see sculptures

You can find sculptures in
many different places, such as . . .

▲ . . . in a museum
or gallery

▲ . . . in a park

Sculpture spotting
Try to spot some sculptures in
different places on your travels.

▲ . . . or in a
temple or church.

Imagine! The nose of this statue is about as big as you are!

◀ **The Statue of Liberty,** **Auguste Bartholdi, 1884**

This famous sculpture is on Liberty Island in New York Harbor. The statue is so big that it can be seen from a great distance.

How do sculptures look?

Some sculptures look like real people, animals, or objects. This style is called **realistic**. Other sculptures are simple shapes and forms. This style is called **abstract**.

▶ **French statue of the Virgin and Child, 14th century**
This is a realistic sculpture. Look at the **detail** of the faces and clothes. These details make the sculpture look very lifelike.

Different styles
Both of these sculptures show a mother and a baby. Which style do you like better? Why?

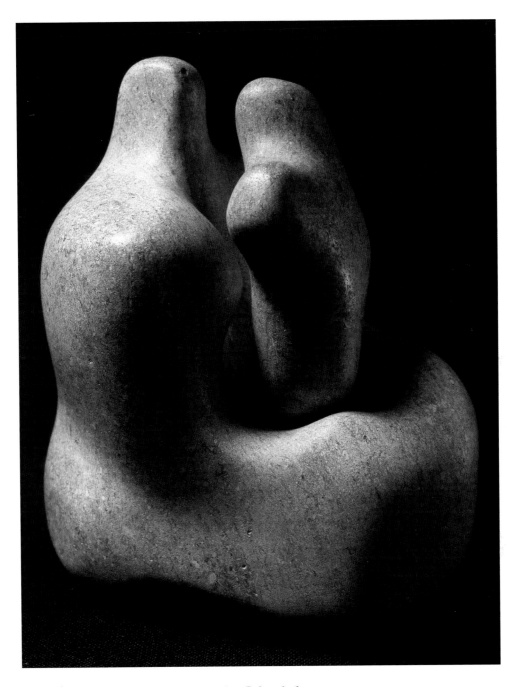

▲ *Mother and Child,*
Barbara Hepworth, 1934
Look at the shapes and curves of this
abstract sculpture. Can you see the
faces, arms, or legs of the two figures?

How do sculptures feel?

The way a sculpture feels is called its **texture**. A sculpture may feel hard or soft, rough or smooth.

Textured tortoise
How would this stone tortoise feel if you touched it?

Feel it
Feel some objects around your house or in your classroom. Use these words to help describe them.

rough   hard   furry   smooth   wet
dry   soft   cold   flat   bumpy   slippery

A real elephant's skin
is wrinkly and rough.
Does this elephant have
the same texture?

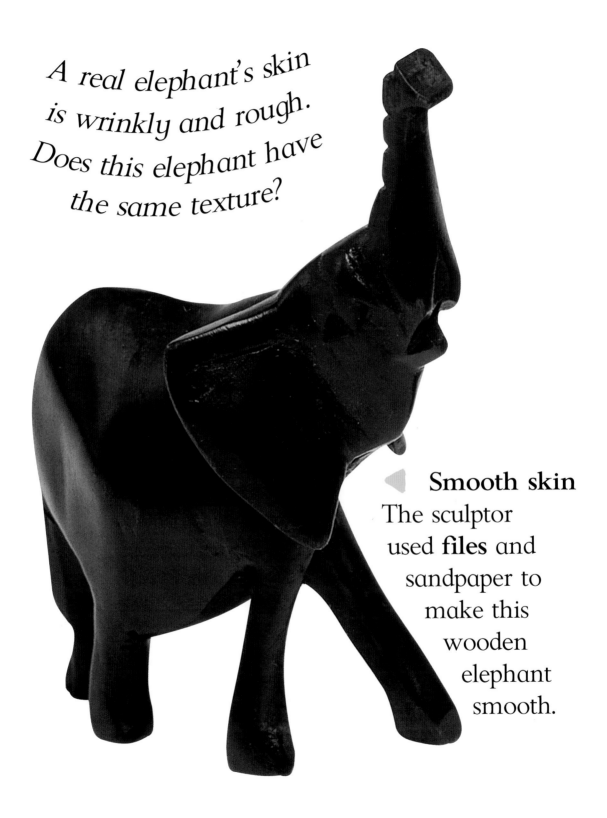

Smooth skin
The sculptor
used **files** and
sandpaper to
make this
wooden
elephant
smooth.

Colorful sculptures

Sometimes sculptors use different colors to paint their sculptures.

Color change
Use modeling clay to make three sculptures that look the same. See how they change when you paint them different colors and patterns.

▲ **Painted mask**
Look at the dark colors of this mask. Do the colors make it look scary or funny to you? Notice the big red eyes and mouth.

14

Look at the water squirting from this sculpture's head.

🔺 *Firebird*, Niki de Saint Phalle, 1983

This colorful sculpture is part of a big fountain. How many colors can you see? How do the colors make you feel?

Modeling

Sometimes sculptors shape soft materials, such as clay or plaster, to make sculptures. This is called **modeling**.

◀ Shaping clay
Sculptors shape the clay with their hands or with special tools. Sometimes the sculpture is baked in a hot oven, called a kiln, to make it hard.

Modeling magic
Use modeling clay to make your own sculpture. Think about how it will look from the front, back, sides, and from above.

How has the sculptor made the eyes of this king and queen?

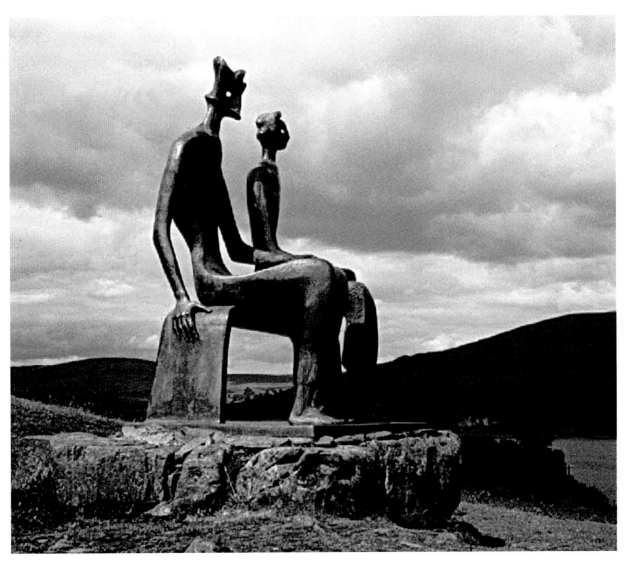

▲ *King and Queen*, Henry Moore, 1952-53

This sculpture is made of bronze. Moore made a small plaster model of it first, called a **maquette**. The maquette gave him an idea of what the big finished sculpture would look like.

Carving

Some sculptures are made by carving away material, such as stone or wood.

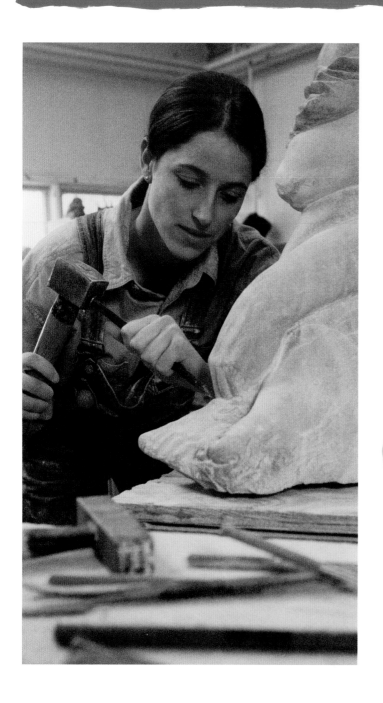

◀ **How to carve**
This sculptor is using a **mallet** and **chisel** to chip away at a big block of stone. When she taps the mallet, the sharp chisel cuts off bits of stone.

How was it made?
When you see a sculpture, look at it carefully. Try to guess what material it is made from and how it was made.

▶ Native American totem pole
This totem pole was carved from the trunk of a tall tree and then painted. Each face on the totem pole is different.

◀ Dancing bear
A sculptor carved this bear from stone. Then he polished it to make it smooth and shiny.

Building sculptures

Sometimes sculptors put objects together to make a sculpture. This is called **constructing**.

▲ Found objects
These colorful sculptures are made from objects the African sculptor found, such as old tin cans, scraps of wire, and plastic telephone cord.

Recycled robot
Look around for things that you can use to make a sculpture. Can you guess what was used to make this robot?

▲ *Balouba III*, Jean Tinguely, 1961
What objects has Tinguely used to
make this sculpture? There is even a
motor that makes the sculpture move.

Natural sculptures

Sculptors also use things they find in nature to make sculptures.

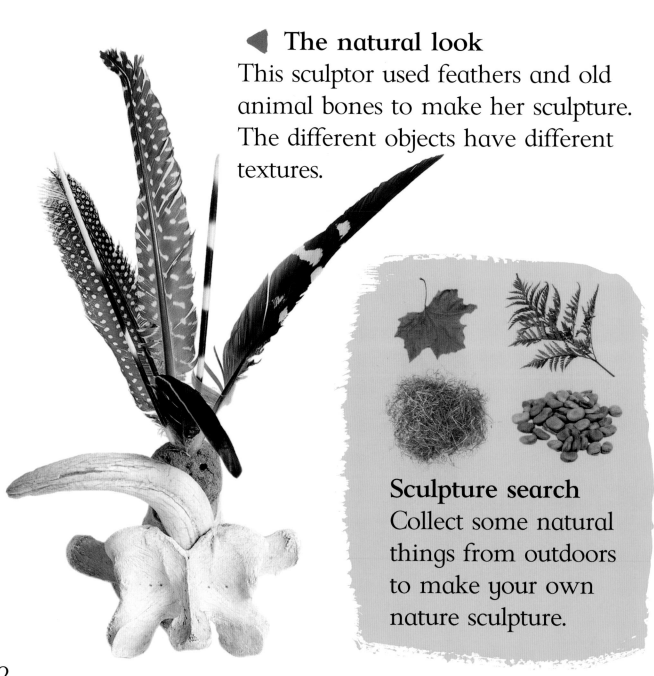

◀ **The natural look**
This sculptor used feathers and old animal bones to make her sculpture. The different objects have different textures.

Sculpture search
Collect some natural things from outdoors to make your own nature sculpture.

Ice star, Andy Goldsworthy, 1987
This sculpture is made of ice.
What do you think happened to it
when the sun shone on it?

Sculptures that move

The sculptures on these pages are hanging sculptures, called mobiles. The wind makes them move.

◀ **Wood turner**
This sculpture is made from lots of thin slats of wood that twist and curve. When the mobile spins quickly, the colors seem to blend together.

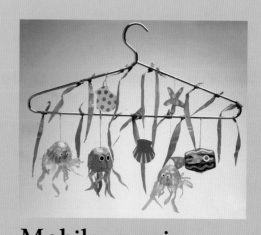

Mobile magic
Use colored paper, thread, and a clothes hanger to make your own mobile.

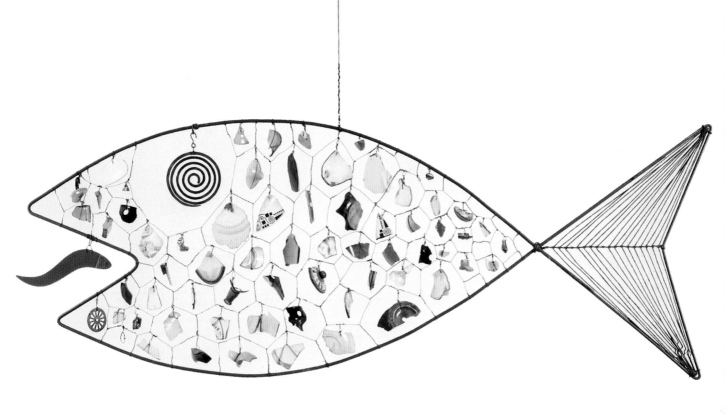

How does the sculptor
make this fish look as if it has scales?

▲ *Brazilian Fish*,
Alexander Calder, 1947
Calder is famous for
making mobiles. He
made this hanging fish
from scraps of metal,
glass, and pottery.

Giant sculptures

Sculptures can be any size.
Some sculptures are enormous.

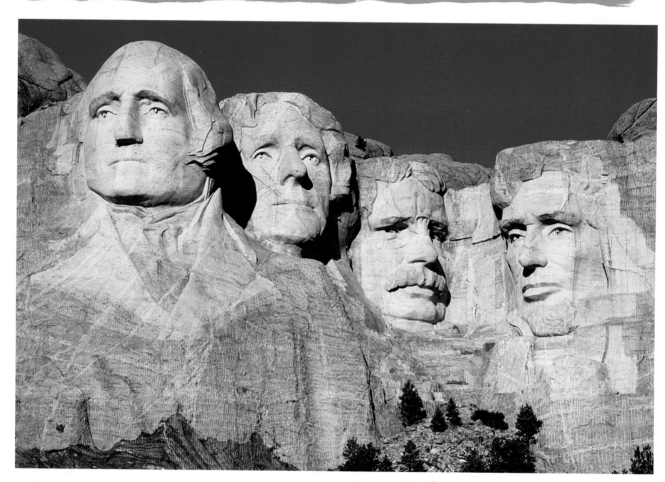

▲*Mount Rushmore,* Gutzon Borglum, 1927-41
Four hundred workers carved this huge sculpture into the side of a rocky mountain.

What's the big idea?
Imagine that you are making a giant sculpture. What would you make? What material would you use? Where would you put it?

▲ *Angel of the North*, Anthony Gormley, 1995-98
This giant angel sculpture is made of metal. It is so big that its feet are as tall as an adult. The sculpture stands near a busy highway, where lots of people see it.

27

Quiz

1. Is this sculpture abstract or realistic? Find more abstract and realistic sculptures in the book.

2. What texture does this sculpture have? Find more sculptures in the book with a similar texture.

3. Find sculptures in the book that are made of wood, stone, or metal.

4. Look through the book to find at least 10 carved sculptures.

5. Was this sculpture modeled or constructed? Look through the book to find other sculptures that have been modeled or constructed.

Glossary

abstract A style of sculpture that is based on line and shape. Abstract sculptures do not usually look lifelike.

bronze A kind of metal that is often used for sculpture.

chisel A tool used for carving wood or stone.

clay A type of earth that is easy to model when it is mixed with water.

constructing Building a sculpture from different objects or materials.

detail The smallest, finest parts of a sculpture that make it look lifelike, such as hairs, veins, or texture.

file A tool used to give stone and wood a smooth finish.

mallet A hammer used to hit the end of a chisel when carving.

maquette A small model that gives a sculptor an idea of what the finished sculpture will look like.

modeling Making a sculpture by shaping a soft material.

realistic A style of sculpture that is made to look lifelike.

texture How things feel, for example, rough or smooth.

Websites

www.sculpture.org
International website with lists of places around the world where sculptures are on display.

www.henry-moore-fdn.co.uk
Information about Henry Moore's life and work, with online galleries.

www.groundsforsculpture.org
A sculpture park containing innovative modern sculptures.

www.sculpturebythesea.com
Online gallery of sculptures from an annual outdoor exhibition in Australia.

Note to parents and teachers
Every effort has been made by the Publishers to ensure that these websites are suitable for children. However, because of the nature of the Internet, it is impossible to guarantee that the contents of these sites will not be altered. We strongly advise that Internet access is supervised by a responsible adult.

Index